Being Kind

By Janine Amos and Annabel Spenceley
Consultant Rachael Underwood

CHERRYTREE BOOKS

VISIT OUR WEBSITE
www.evansbooks.co.uk

A Cherrytree book

Designed and produced by
A S Publishing

Published by Cherrytree Press, a division of Evans Publishing Group
2A Portman Mansions
Chiltern St
London W1U 6NR

Reprinted 2006

British Library Cataloguing in Publication Data
Amos, Janine
        Being Kind. - (Growing Up)
        1. Kindness - Juvenile literature
        1. Title
        177.7

        ISBN 1 84234 005 0
        ISBN (from 1 Jan 2007) 978 1 84234 005 9

Printed in Malaysia

Rachel and Zoë

Green. Yellow. Purple.

Everyone's busy painting.

It's Rachel's first day at school.
How does Rachel feel?

"Where can I work?" Rachel
wonders.

Zoë looks up. She sees Rachel.

She smiles at her.

Zoë puts down her brush.
"I'll show you where the things
are," she says.

"Here's the paper," says Zoë.

"And here's an apron."

Zoë helps Rachel to put on her apron.

"You can work next to me,"
says Zoë.

Dave hurries across. "You found everything!" he says.
"Zoë showed me," Rachel tells him.

Dave turns to Zoë.
"You helped Rachel get started.
That was kind," he says.

Daniel and Ryan

Here are the hats. Here are
the cloaks.

The children are dressing up.

"I'm a pirate!" laughs Daniel.

Ryan looks at him.

"I'm a wizard!" calls Megan.

Ryan feels worried.

Josh pulls on a green cloak.

"I'm a dragon!" he shouts. "Grr! Grr!"

Daniel watches Ryan.

Ryan is scared.

Daniel goes over to Ryan.

He stands right next to him.

Daniel takes hold of Ryan's hand.

He smiles at Ryan.
And Ryan feels safe.

There are lots of ways to be kind to people. Notice if someone is looking worried or alone. You can be kind to them by going over to them.

You can talk to them.
You can stay with them if they're feeling upset.
Being kind to someone shows you care.